THE TWELVE APOSTLES OF JESUS CHRIST: LESSONS WE CAN LEARN

Bisi Oladipupo

Copyright © 2021 by Bisi Oladipupo

All Rights Reserved.

No part of this book may be used or reproduced by any means, graphic, electronic, or mechanical, including photocopying, recording, taping, or by any information storage retrieval system without the written permission of the publisher except in the case of brief quotations embodied in critical articles and reviews.

Printed in the United Kingdom

Table of Contents

Dedication iv

Foreword v

How did Jesus choose the twelve Apostles? vi

Andrew 1

Bartholomew 2

James the son of Alphaeus 3

James the brother of John 4

John the brother of James 5

Judas the brother of James 8

Judas Iscariot 10

Matthew 14

Philip 15

Simon Peter 16

Simon the Zealot 19

Thomas 20

Conclusion 23

Salvation prayer 24

About the author 25

Dedication

To Jesus Christ, my Lord and Saviour—to Him alone that laid down His life that 1 might have life eternal. To Him that led captivity captive and gave gifts unto men (Ephesians 4:8). One of those gifts is writing!

Bisi Oladipupo

Foreword

This short book will look at the life of the twelve disciples of the Lamb, known as the twelve apostles of our Lord Jesus Christ, during His earthly ministry.

The piece of work will only look at scriptures and not any other historical findings.

As some of the disciples have more revealed about them in scriptures than others, this indicates that l will not be able to go in-depth with all the disciples.

2 Timothy 3:16-17 reads, "*All scripture is given by inspiration of God, and is profitable for doctrine, for reproof, for correction, for instruction in righteousness: That the man of God may be perfect, thoroughly furnished unto all good works*".

As this is the case, there is a reason we have a bit more account of some of the disciples than others.

As you read this book, I trust that you will learn from the lives of the twelve apostles of the Lamb.

Shalom!

Bisi Oladipupo

How Did Jesus Choose The Twelve Apostles?

The first place to start would be to find out how our Lord Jesus Christ chose His disciples. This can be found in the gospels.

Some of the disciples had a hunger already present in their hearts to find Jesus Christ before becoming the Lord's disciples. Therefore, it can be assumed that they must have searched the scriptures. Why can we say that?

Let's look at the Book of John.

John knew who he was. He made it clear to those that came to ask him that he was not the Christ (John 1:20). John made it clear that he was the one sent to prepare the way of the Lord: *"I am the voice of one crying in the wilderness, make straight the way of the Lord, as said the prophet Esaias"* (John 1:23). In John 1:34, John declared: *"And I saw, and bare record that this is the Son of God"*.

After this account, the scriptures tell us that the next day, John declared this again. He declared who Jesus was. However, on this occasion, two of John's disciples were with him. John 1:35-42 reads, *"Again the next day after John stood, and two of his disciples; and looking upon Jesus as he walked, he saith, Behold the Lamb of God! And the two disciples heard him speak, and they followed Jesus. Then Jesus turned, and saw them following, and saith unto them, what seek ye? They said unto him, Rabbi, (which is to say, being interpreted, Master,) where dwellest thou? He saith unto them, Come and see. They came and saw where he dwelt, and abode with him that day: for it was about the tenth hour. One of the two which heard John speak, and followed him, was Andrew, Simon Peter's brother. He first findeth his own brother Simon, and saith unto him, we have found the Messias, which is, being interpreted, the Christ. And he brought him to Jesus. And when Jesus beheld him, he said, thou art Simon the son of Jona: thou shalt be called Cephas, which is by interpretation, A stone".*

As we can see from this account, once the two disciples heard from John that Jesus was the Lamb of God, they left John and followed Jesus Christ. This shows that they had been searching for Jesus Christ. A work was already going on in their hearts. Once they found Jesus, there was no discussion. They didn't even get permission from John; they just left John and followed Jesus Christ.

The scripture says, "For it is God which worketh in you both to will and to do of his good pleasure" (Philippians 2:13).

What is the Lord doing in your heart? What desires are on the inside from the Lord? Don't dismiss it; you have no idea why the Lord placed those desires in your heart. It's very unlikely that these two former disciples of John knew that their desire to find the Messiah would one day result in them becoming one of the apostles of Jesus Christ. *Sometimes, destiny starts with a simple longing or desire.*

John 1:43-47 reads,

"The day following Jesus would go forth into Galilee, and findeth Philip, and saith unto him, Follow me. Now Philip was of Bethsaida, the city of Andrew and Peter. Philip findeth Nathanael, and saith unto him, we have found him, of whom Moses in the law, and the prophets, did write, Jesus of Nazareth, the son of Joseph. And Nathanael said unto him, Can there any good thing come out of Nazareth? Philip saith unto him, Come and see. Jesus saw Nathanael coming to him, and saith of him, Behold an Israelite indeed, in whom is no guile!"

So, we can see from the above account that Jesus already had disciples. Of course, we don't know how many disciples Jesus Christ had; however, one thing is sure; Jesus chose the twelve apostles from His disciples.

Here, we can see that Jesus went to find Philip, and then Philip went to find Nathanael. Once again, we can see that Philip had a hunger and was looking for the Messiah as we can find his statement in verse 45: *"We have found him, of whom Moses in the law, and the prophets, did write, Jesus of Nazareth, the son of Joseph"*.

We don't know if Nathanael became a disciple of Jesus Christ, but if he did, he was not chosen as one of the twelve.

In other parts of the gospel, we can see that Jesus had disciples before He chose the twelve from them.

In the Book of Luke chapter 5, we have an account of where Simon Peter was told to launch into the deep to catch fish. Peter responded that they had toiled all night; nevertheless, he will let down the net at the word of the Lord.

This account can be found in Luke 5:1-7.

This is Simon Peter's response after the multitude of fish were caught:

"When Simon Peter saw it, he fell down at Jesus' knees, saying, depart from me; for I am a sinful man, O Lord. For he was astonished, and all that were with him, at the draught of the fishes which they had taken: And so was also **James, and John, the sons of Zebedee**, which were partners with Simon. And Jesus said unto Simon, Fear not; from henceforth thou shalt catch men. **And when they had brought their ships to land, they forsook all, and followed him"** (Luke 5:8-11).

This account shows that they had not yet been called as apostles of Jesus Christ. This can be confirmed from verse 11, **"And when they had brought their ships to land, they forsook all, and followed him."**

Jesus Christ prayed before He chose the twelve apostles from the disciples He already had.

Let us look at this from scripture:

"And it came to pass in those days, that he went out into a mountain to pray, and continued all night in prayer to God. And when it was day, **he called unto him his disciples: and of them he chose twelve, whom also he named apostles;** Simon, (whom he also named Peter,) and Andrew his brother, James and John, Philip and Bartholomew, Matthew and Thomas, James the son of Alphaeus, and Simon called Zelotes, And Judas the brother of James, and Judas Iscariot, which also was the traitor" (Luke 6:12-16).

So, here, we can see that Jesus called His disciples and chose twelve whom He named apostles.

In the Book of Acts, we can also find the names of the twelve apostles minus Judas Iscariot. "And when they were come in, they went up into an upper room, where abode both Peter, and James, and John, and Andrew, Philip, and Thomas, Bartholomew, and Matthew, James the son of Alphaeus, and Simon Zelotes, and Judas the brother of James" (Acts 1:13).

We don't have much background on some of them, but at least, at the time they were chosen, they were all disciples of Jesus Christ.

Jesus Christ had some relationship with the disciples before the twelve were chosen from them. This is a natural process and why it is important to stay hooked up with those that God brings across our paths. *You have no idea where the relationship will lead to*. Some connections are God-ordained. *Relationships are important. Value those that the Lord places in your life.*

Keep your God-ordained relationships. Jesus Christ, our Lord, chose His apostles from those that were already following Him.

Now, let us look at the lives of each disciple and see what we can learn from them.

Andrew

Andrew was Simon Peter's brother (Matthew 4:18). It also looks like Andrew and Simon Peter, for a period, lived together (Mark 1:29).

Andrew was initially a disciple of John, and when he heard John say that Jesus Christ is the Lamb of God, Andrew left John the Baptist and followed Jesus.

We don't have much said about Andrew in scripture, but from how Andrew found the Lord, we can assume that he was looking for the Messiah as he left John and followed Jesus Christ (John 1:40-41).

Bartholomew

Bartholomew is another of the twelve apostles of Jesus Christ that we don't know anything about. All we know is his name (Mark 3:18; Luke 6:14) and that he was also present at the upper room waiting for the promise of the Holy Spirit (Acts 1:13-14).

This simply means that not everyone's ministry is going to be publicly known here on earth, but as it has been stated before, this has nothing to do with our eternal rewards.

Has the Lord called you to a work that nobody seems to know about? Remember that not all the twelve apostles of our Lord Jesus Christ had great works credited to their names in scripture. But as they were called apostles, they all played their part in the foundation of the Body of Christ today, and all have reaped eternal rewards.

"And are built upon the foundation of the apostles and prophets, Jesus Christ himself being the chief corner stone" (Ephesians 2:20).

James the son of Alphaeus

This is another one of the twelve disciples of Jesus Christ called "apostles" that we also don't know too much about.

He was one of the twelve (Luke 6:15; Matthew 10:3) and also at the upper room (Acts 1:13).

Once again, we can see an unsung earthly hero that has been given a great reward in heaven (Revelation 21:14).

James the brother of John

Our Lord Jesus Christ had two apostles called James. James the son of Zebedee (also referred to as the brother of John) and James the son of Alphaeus (Mark 3:17; Luke 5:10, and Acts 12:2).

James, the brother of John was one of the three disciples that followed Jesus when Jesus went to raise the ruler of the synagogue's daughter from the dead (Mark 5:37). He also experienced the transfiguration of the Lord (Mark 9:2), and Jesus took him up with two other disciples to the Garden of Gethsemane, where Jesus prayed before He was betrayed (Mark 14:33).

From this account, we can see that James, the brother of John, was one of the three inner-circle disciples of the Lord Jesus Christ.

James, the brother of John, alongside his brother John, asked if they could sit on the right hand and left hand in His glory (Mark 10:37).

James is one of the disciples that the Bible expressly showed how he died. James was killed by Herod.

"Now about that time Herod the king stretched forth his hands to vex certain of the church. And he killed James the brother of John with the sword" (Acts 12:1-2).

So, what can we learn from James the brother of John? First, he has his eternal reward in heaven like the others did. Second, he died a martyr for the Lord Jesus Christ.

John the brother of James

John was also referred to as "the disciple whom Jesus loved" in some places in scripture. From scripture, we get the impression that John was closer to the Lord Jesus Christ than the other disciples. Yes, Jesus Christ loved all His disciples, but it appears that some of them had a closer walk than others.

A good example of this can be seen where Jesus took only three of His disciples along with Him when He went to raise Jarius' daughter from the dead. Nevertheless, these same three disciples experienced the transfiguration of the Lord, and they were also in the Garden of Gethsemane when Jesus went to pray before His crucifixion (Mark 5:37; Mark 9:2, and Mark 14:33). Amongst these three was John the brother of James.

What gives us the further impression that John was closer to the Lord can be found first in the description of John as "the disciple whom Jesus loved".

We found one expression when our Lord Jesus Christ revealed to His disciples that one of them would betray Him. It is said that Peter then asked the disciple leaning on Jesus' bosom, "the disciple whom Jesus loved", who it was that would betray Him.

Why did Peter himself not ask the Lord?

"Now there was leaning on Jesus' bosom one of his disciples, whom Jesus loved. Simon Peter therefore beckoned to him, that he should ask who it should be of whom he spake. He then lying on Jesus' breast saith unto him, Lord, who is it? Jesus answered, He it is, to whom I shall give a sop, when I have dipped it. And when he had dipped the sop, he gave it to Judas Iscariot, the son of Simon" (John 13:23-26).

We can also find another account that indicates that this disciple was close to the Lord.

When Jesus Christ was on the cross, He handed over His mother to John.

John 19:25-27:

"Now there stood by the cross of Jesus his mother, and his mother's sister, Mary the wife of Cleophas, and Mary Magdalene. When Jesus therefore saw his mother, and the disciple standing by, whom he loved, he saith unto his mother, Woman, behold thy son! Then saith he to the disciple, Behold thy mother! And from that hour that disciple took her unto his own home" (John 19:25-27).

History says that John wrote the Book of John. It is very clear from scripture that John wrote the Book of Revelation.

"The Revelation of Jesus Christ, which God gave unto him, to shew unto his servants things which must shortly come to pass; and he sent and signified it by his angel unto his servant John" (Revelation 1:1).

"I John, who also am your brother, and companion in tribulation, and in the kingdom and patience of Jesus Christ, was in the isle that is called Patmos, for the word of God, and for the testimony of Jesus Christ" (Revelation 1:9).

It is also believed that John wrote the Book of 1 John, 2 John, and 3 John. So, is it any surprise that John, known as "the disciple whom Jesus loved", writes about the love of God in 1 John 4:7-8? Could this have been a progressive revelation of God's love for him and us? I don't think that it is a coincidence that the one that knew he was loved wrote about the love of God.

We can see from scripture that each apostle had their individual walk with the Lord to fulfil the role of an apostle.

For John, it was intimacy, "the disciple whom Jesus loved", writing the Books of 1 John to 3 John and that of Revelation—the last book of the Bible.

Judas the brother of James

Our Lord Jesus Christ had two apostles amongst the twelve called Judas. Judas the brother of James (Luke 6:16) and Judas Iscariot.

Judas the brother of James, was also known as Lebbaeus, whose surname was Thaddaeus (Matthew 10:3) and just also recorded as Thaddaeus (Mark 3:18).

We don't have much said about Judas the brother of James. All we know is that he asked Jesus Christ a question.

In the Book of John, Jesus is speaking to His disciples:

"He that hath my commandments, and keepeth them, he it is that loveth me: and he that loveth me shall be loved of my Father, and I will love him, and will manifest myself to him. **Judas saith unto him, not Iscariot, Lord, how is it that thou wilt manifest thyself unto us, and not unto the world?** Jesus answered and said unto him, If a man love me, he will keep my words: and my Father will love him, and we will come unto him, and make our abode with him" (John 14:21-23).

What can we learn from this?

Not being known on earth does not change our reward in heaven. Although Judas the brother of James was only mentioned a few times in scriptures, it does not change his eternal reward being one of the twelve apostles of the Lamb.

Revelation 21:14 reads,

"And the wall of the city had twelve foundations, and in them the names of the twelve apostles of the Lamb".

Judas the brother of James is one of the names that will remain on the corridors of the foundation of the New Jerusalem for eternity.

"Not being popular on earth has nothing to do with your eternal rewards". Just stay faithful to what the Lord has called you to do. It might be in secret, but heaven sees it.

Judas Iscariot

Judas Iscariot was one the twelve apostles of Jesus Christ who betrayed Him.

In today's society, not much is said about Judas Iscariot; however, many lessons can be learned from this disciple.

Our God is good; God is gracious and faithful. The Bible says that God is love (1 John 4:7).

God has given man free will, and man can decide to use their will as they so please. We know the enemy's main tool is deception (Revelation 12: 9). This is why we must guard our hearts (Proverbs 4:23) and be careful with who and what we associate with.

Loving the Lord should be the first priority of every believer (Mark 12:30). We are also told to fear God (1 Peter 2:7). Proverbs 14:23 reads, *"The fear of the LORD is a fountain of life, to depart from the snares of death"*.

What eventually happened to Judas was his own choice. This is the Lord's will for all those who come to Him: "And this is the Father's will which hath sent me, that of all which he hath given me I should lose nothing, but should raise it up again at the last day" (John 6:39).

It is just like the Lord who would have all men to be saved. 1 Timothy 2:4 reads, *"Who will have all men to be saved, and to come unto the knowledge of the truth"*.

Once we are saved, we live our lives for Him, through Him, and to bring Him glory. After all, the Lord has done so much for us. The wise live one hundred percent for the Lord. This world is temporal, and what we do now will determine our eternity and eternal rewards.

Now, let us go back to Judas Iscariot.

I think it is safe to say that Judas Iscariot had some heart issues that he never dealt with. Judas never judged himself, and this allowed the enemy to use him.

Now, let us see some traits of Judas Iscariot before he betrayed the Lord.

The Lord Jesus Christ raised Lazarus from the dead after he had been dead for four days. This account can be found in John chapter 11.

Subsequently, Jesus Christ was at supper with Martha (Lazarus's sister), and Lazarus was one of the guests.

In appreciation of our Lord Jesus Christ, and it could also be for gratitude to Jesus Christ for raising her brother Lazarus from the dead, Mary anointed Jesus Christ's feet with costly ointment. Let us look at the account and see Judas Iscariot's response.

"Then Jesus six days before the passover came to Bethany, where Lazarus was, which had been dead, whom he raised from the dead. There they made him a supper; and Martha served: but Lazarus was one of them that sat at the table with him.Then took Mary a pound of ointment of spikenard, very costly, and anointed the feet of Jesus, and wiped his feet with her hair: and the house was filled with the odour of the ointment. **Then saith one of his disciples, Judas Iscariot, Simon's son, which should betray him, Why was not this ointment sold for three hundred pence, and given to the poor? This he said, not that he cared for the poor; but because he was a thief, and had the bag, and bare what was put therein.** Then said Jesus, Let her alone: against the day of my burying hath she kept this" (John 12:1-7).

We can see from this account that Judas Iscariot had a greed problem. The Bible clearly states that he did not care for the poor, but he was a thief and stole from the bag.

So, why did Judas Iscariot have the bag? John 13:29 also confirms that Judas Iscariot oversaw the bag. Did our Lord Jesus Christ not know that he was a thief?

I think it is safe to say that the bag was his test. Judas Iscariot being responsible for the bag was simply a way for him to judge himself. It was simply a test.

Judas Iscariot never judged himself, neither did he judge his heart, and the enemy took advantage of that.

Now, let us see other traits of Judas Iscariot from scripture.

"Now before the feast of the passover, when Jesus knew that his hour was come that he should depart out of this world unto the Father, having loved his own which were in the world, he loved them unto the end. And supper being ended, the devil having now put into the heart of Judas Iscariot, Simon's son, to betray him; Jesus knowing that the Father had given all things into his hands, and that he was come from God, and went to God; He riseth from supper, and laid aside his garments; and took a towel, and girded himself. After that he poureth water into a bason, and began to wash the disciples' feet, and to wipe them with the towel wherewith he was girded. Then cometh he to Simon Peter: and Peter saith unto him, Lord, dost thou wash my feet? Jesus answered and said unto him, What I do thou knowest not now; but thou shalt know hereafter. Peter saith unto him, thou shalt never wash my feet. Jesus answered him, If I wash thee not, thou hast no part with me. Simon Peter saith unto him, Lord, not my feet only, but also my hands and my head. Jesus saith to him, He that is washed needeth not save to wash his feet, but is clean every whit: and ye are clean, but not all. For he knew who should betray him; therefore said he, Ye are not all clean. **So after he had washed their feet, and had taken his garments, and was set down again, he said unto them, know ye what I have done to you?"** (John 13:1-12)

This scripture shows that Jesus Christ washed all the disciples' feet, including Judas Iscariot's. Judas Iscariot did not judge himself.

Did Jesus Christ our Lord make a mistake in choosing Judas Iscariot? Did our Lord Jesus Christ not pray before choosing His disciples?

Our Lord Jesus Christ did not make a mistake, and we know that Jesus Christ prayed before He chose and called them apostles. Judas Iscariot made his own decisions. He was given opportunities to judge himself, and he did not.

Judas Iscariot forfeited God's great plan for this life.

Matthew

Matthew is another one of the twelve apostles of the Lord Jesus Christ (Mark 3:18; Luke 6:15). Matthew was formally a tax collector and then called.

"And as Jesus passed forth from thence, he saw a man, named Matthew, sitting at the receipt of custom: and he saith unto him, Follow me. And he arose, and followed him" (Matthew 9:8).

We also know that Matthew was amongst the apostles who waited for the promise of the Holy Spirit in the Book of Acts chapter one.

Tradition states that Matthew wrote the Book of Matthew.

Philip

Philip is another one of the twelve apostles that not much is said about. It was Philip that the Lord asked: *where shall we buy bread for this many to eat*? Philip answered two hundred pennyworths of bread is not sufficient for them, that every one of them may take a little (John 6:5-7).

It was Philip who also asked Jesus, *"Lord, show us the father and it sufficeth us"* (John 14:8).

Not much is said about Philip; however, as mentioned before, Philip may not have been known on earth, but his eternal rewards remain for being an apostle of the Lord.

Simon Peter

Many of us are aware of Simon Peter because he was the disciple that denied the Lord three times even though he was warned.

From the account of the denial, we can tell that Peter did love the Lord. Why can we say that? Because Peter was the only disciple that followed the Lord afar off when Jesus was arrested. All the others fled!

"In that same hour said Jesus to the multitudes, Are ye come out as against a thief with swords and staves for to take me? I sat daily with you teaching in the temple, and ye laid no hold on me. But all this was done, that the scriptures of the prophets might be fulfilled. **Then all the disciples forsook him, and fled.** And they that had laid hold on Jesus led him away to Caiaphas the high priest, where the scribes and the elders were assembled. **But Peter followed him afar off unto the high priest's palace, and went in, and sat with the servants, to see the end**" (Matthew 26:55-58).

Peter loved the Lord; otherwise, he would have fled like the others did. The enemy took advantage of a weakness in Peter's character, which appears to be the fear of man. There is a repeat of the fear of man displayed by Peter in the Book of Galatians, where Peter withdrew himself because of the fear of the circumcision.

"But when Peter was come to Antioch, I withstood him to the face, because he was to be blamed. For before that certain came from James, he did eat with the Gentiles: but when they were come, he withdrew and separated himself,

fearing them which were of the circumcision" (Galatians 2:11-12).

What can we learn from this? We are all work in progress and the Lord can still use us with our issues.

From the account of scriptures, we can tell that Peter was quite outspoken. He seems to be the disciple that asked most of the questions and also answered questions.

Peter was the only disciple that asked if he could walk on water (Matthew 14:28).

When Jesus asked His disciples about His real identity and what men say about Him, only Peter answered: *thou art the Christ; the Son of the living God* (Matthew 16:15-16).

When Jesus took Peter, James, and John up the high mountain and He was transfigured in their presence, it was Peter that spoke:

"And after six days Jesus taketh Peter, James, and John his brother, and bringeth them up into an high mountain apart, and was transfigured before them: and his face did shine as the sun, and his raiment was white as the light. And, behold, there appeared unto them Moses and Elias talking with him. **Then answered Peter, and said unto Jesus**, Lord, it is good for us to be here: if thou wilt, let us make here three tabernacles; one for thee, and one for Moses, and one for Elias" (Matthew 17:1-4).

It was Peter that asked how many times he should forgive a person (Matthew 18:29).

It was Peter that asked what their reward shall be since they have left all (Matthew 19:27).

These are just a few of Peter's statements in the gospels.

After Jesus died and rose from the dead, we can see Peter in another light. It was Peter that the Lord used to heal the lame man that had not walked in over 40 years. Both Peter and John saw the lame man, but it was Peter that spoke to the situation (Acts 3:6). It was Peter's shadow that healed the sick (Acts 5:15). It was Peter that spoke when Ananias held back part of the money he and his wife sold their land for and lied (Acts 5:3-8). Peter raised Dorcas back to life (Acts 9:36-40).

Peter also wrote some books in the New Testament (1 Peter and 2 Peter).

So, what can we learn from the life of Peter?

Peter was used mightily of the Lord; yet, the enemy tried to sift him as wheat had the Lord not prayed for him.

Peter had a great destiny in the Lord, and thank God that he fulfilled it. The Lord knew Peter's heart, and though he denied Jesus thrice, the Lord saw his heart.

"We must never judge people by their actions as only the Lord sees the heart. We must restore our brethren that fall just as Jesus restored Peter".

Simon the Zealot

Simon the Zealot was one of the twelve disciples of the Lord Jesus Christ (Luke 6:15). He was also known as Simon the Canaanite (Mark 3:18 & Matthew 10:4).

He is another one of the disciples that we don't know much about but followed the Lord during His earthly ministry as one of the twelve.

Thomas

We don't have much account about Thomas in the Bible. However, one thing we know about Thomas is that he tends to doubt.

Isn't it interesting that Jesus' disciples were just everyday people? None of them dropped from heaven, and the Lord had a great destiny for each of them. This shows us that whatever defects we found in our flesh, we must mortify them through the Spirit (Romans 8:13).

Isn't it also interesting to know that the Lord had eternal rewards for every one of them? At least, we can see a few in scripture.

Matthew 19:27-28 reads,

"Then answered Peter and said unto him, Behold, we have forsaken all, and followed thee; what shall we have therefore? And Jesus said unto them, Verily I say unto you, That ye which have followed me, in the regeneration when the Son of man shall sit in the throne of his glory, ye also shall sit upon twelve thrones, judging the twelve tribes of Israel".

This is one reward the apostles had—to sit upon twelve thrones judging the twelve tribes of Israel.

We can see another reward in the Book of Revelation describing part of the New Jerusalem:

"And the wall of the city had twelve foundations, and in them the names of the twelve apostles of the Lamb" (Revelation 21:14).

We need to look beyond our flesh; the Lord has great plans and rewards for us. Don't allow anyone to put you in a box. We must remember that the Lord is no respecter of persons. The Lord wants to work through us all.

Now, let us look at Thomas.

As stated, Thomas had a tendency to doubt. When Jesus Christ heard that Lazarus was dead, Jesus had already said that He was going to raise Lazarus:

"These things said he: and after that he saith unto them, Our friend Lazarus sleepeth; but I go, that I may awake him out of sleep. Then said his disciples, Lord, if he sleep, he shall do well. Howbeit Jesus spake of his death: but they thought that he had spoken of taking of rest in sleep. Then said Jesus unto them plainly, Lazarus is dead. And I am glad for your sakes that I was not there, to the intent ye may believe; nevertheless let us go unto him" (John 11:11-15).

Now, let us look at Thomas' response:

"Then said Thomas, which is called Didymus, unto his fellow disciples, let us also go, that we may die with him" (John 11:16).

That doesn't sound like a statement of faith. We can see that Thomas tends to doubt.

We can see another account in the Book of John where Jesus Christ told His disciples that they knew where He was going, and they knew the way:

"In my Father's house are many mansions: if it were not so, I would have told you. I go to prepare a place for you. And if I go and prepare a place for you, I will come again, and receive you unto myself; that where I am, there ye may be also. And whither I go ye know, and the way ye know" (John 14:2-4).

Now, let us see Thomas' response:

"Thomas saith unto him, Lord, we know not whither thou goest; and how can we know the way? Jesus saith unto him, I am the way, the truth, and the life: no man cometh unto the Father, but by me" (John 14:5-6).

Finally, when Jesus Christ rose from the dead, the others told Thomas, but he refused to believe.

"But Thomas, one of the twelve, called Didymus, was not with them when Jesus came. The other disciples therefore said unto him, we have seen the LORD. But he said unto them, except I shall see in his hands the print of the nails, and put my finger into the print of the nails, and thrust my hand into his side, I will not believe. And after eight days again his disciples were within, and Thomas with them: then came Jesus, the doors being shut, and stood in the midst, and said, Peace be unto you. Then saith he to Thomas, Reach hither thy finger, and behold my hands; and reach hither thy hand, and thrust it into my side: and be not faithless, but believing. And Thomas answered and said unto him, My LORD and my God. Jesus saith unto him, Thomas, because thou hast seen me, thou hast believed: blessed are they that have not seen, and yet have believed" (John 20:24-29).

We can see that Thomas had always tended to doubt. The Lord told Thomas not to be faithless but believing!

We are believers, and this is what Christians do. We believe.

"And blessed is she that believed: for there shall be a performance of those things which were told her from the Lord" (Luke 1:45).

Conclusion

From scripture, we can see that our Lord Jesus Christ had many disciples, but only twelve of them were chosen and called apostles (Luke 6:13).

These apostles were part of the foundation of the church (Ephesians 2:20), and what is interesting is that part of their reward was their names being on the foundation walls in heaven.

"And are built upon the foundation of the apostles and prophets, Jesus Christ himself being the chief corner stone" (Ephesians 2:20).

"And the wall of the city had twelve foundations, and in them the names of the twelve apostles of the Lamb" (Revelation 21:14).

Each apostle had a different role; some were known while others were unknown, but this did not stop their eternal rewards.

We cannot compare ourselves with others; we must stay in our lane and do what the Lord has called each one of us to do.

The twelve apostles of the Lord were human beings like you and me. They had their flaws but did great work for the Lord.

We can learn so much that this treasure is indeed hidden in earthen vessels (2 Corinthians 4:7).

So, let each one of us be committed to engaging with the Lord and do what He has called us to do.

Salvation Prayer

Father God, l come to you in Jesus' name. I admit that I am a sinner, and l now receive the sacrifice that Jesus Christ paid for me.

I confess with my mouth the Lord Jesus, and l believe in my heart that God raised Him from the dead.

I now declare that Jesus Christ is my Lord and Saviour.

Thank you, Father, for saving me in Jesus' name.

I am now your child. Amen.

If you've said this prayer for the first time, send an email to bisiwriter@outlook.com. Start reading your Bible and ask the Lord to guide you to a good church.

About the Author

Bisi Oladipupo has been a Christian for many years and lives in the United Kingdom with her family.

Bisi has attended a few Bible colleges and has recently graduated from Charis Bible College Walsall (June 2021). She is a teacher of God's Words and has a YouTube channel found at https://www.youtube.com/c/BisiOladipupo123

She writes regularly, and her website is www.inspiredwords.org

You can contact Bisi by email at bisiwriter@outlook.com.

QR Code for Bisi's Linktree:

Printed in Great Britain
by Amazon